KT-177-321

Rhiwbina
Cardiff CF14 6HL
Tel: 029 20623732

The Masai
Tribe of Warriors

Contents

Written and photographed
by Jonathan and Angela Scott

Collins

The Masai people

Many years ago in Africa, a warlike race of unusually tall, slim people travelled the Nile into what is now Kenya and Tanzania. They were the Masai – the people who speak the Maa language. Wherever they went, they were respected for their courage and strength as warriors. Today, the Masai are still famous for their independence, their pride in traditions and their way of life.

Dressed in traditional clothes, the Masai are easy to spot because they usually wear red and the young men wear their hair in long, plaited braids.

Masai men have a cloak called a shuka tied at the shoulder, leather sandals on their feet and they carry a spear with a metal tip, or a short wooden club. They are used to walking huge distances in the heat over the African plains, herding their cattle.

Both Masai men and women wear metal earrings and beadwork. The women wear gorgeous circular necklaces, strings of beads and rows of metal bracelets. The men often wear a chain of beadwork on each shoulder. The pattern of the beads can show what **clan** a man is from and even what age he is.

a Masai woman wearing beaded necklaces

Women wear brightly-patterned cloaks in red or blue and have very short hair or shaved heads. They stand very straight and look beautiful in the patterned beadwork necklaces that they wear for **ceremonies**. Ceremonies play a big part in Masai life and both men and women take pride in making sure that they are carried out properly.

Masai history

Today, there are about 350,000 Masai in Kenya and Tanzania, but wherever they live, they are Masai first and foremost and proud of it.

Cattle are at the centre of a Masai's life. "I hope your cattle are well" is a common greeting. According to Masai legend the Masai god Ngai, whose name means "sky", was once part of the Earth. When Earth and sky separated, Ngai sent down cattle to the Masai and from then onwards, all cattle belonged to them.

In the past, many Masai believed that they had the right to steal cattle from non-Masai and they had a **reputation** as cattle rustlers. A young man would raid herds belonging to neighbouring tribes as a way of proving himself a warrior. In modern times, severe punishment for cattle stealing has helped to control the situation and cattle rustling is considered a very serious offence.

Cattle are central to the lives of the Masai.
Young warriors like this one play a vital part
in protecting their tribe's herds.

Over 200 years ago when Europeans came to Africa, they feared the Masai, who had the reputation of being unbeaten in battle. Even today, the three peaks of one of the highest mountains in Africa, Mount Kenya, are named after three famous Masai: Nelion, Lenana and Batian.

But the Masai fought amongst themselves and the British **authorities** in Kenya tricked them into handing over a lot of their land to the newcomers. Their cattle caught diseases from the cattle brought in by the new settlers and the Masai themselves became sick from European illnesses like influenza, measles and smallpox. But the Masai continued to travel about with their cattle, and took little notice of the new borders drawn up by the authorities between Kenya and Tanzania.

How the Masai use their land

Although they will kill any animals that attack their cattle, like lions and hyenas, Masai don't kill wild animals for food. Sheep, goats, a few donkeys and their precious cattle give them almost everything they need. In the past, if there was a bad drought and cattle died, Masai might have been forced to eat **eland** or buffalo, but this happened very rarely. As a result, their lands have always been full of wild animals – antelopes, elephants and rhinos – and even today, the very best wildlife parks in East Africa are part of what was once their land.

Masai herdsmen move their livestock to water each day.

In the past, the Masai didn't grow vegetables because they believed that grassland was sacred and should be used only for cattle. Grass should not be dug up and replaced with maize or potatoes.

In the same way, the Masai weren't interested in owning land. In their eyes, the land was like the air and was owned by everyone. They didn't understand how it could be fenced off into little plots.

Depending on the season, the Masai have always moved about the African plains with their animals looking for fresh grass. Their cattle can live on land that's dry for most of the year, because they only stay in one spot while the grass lasts. As soon as it's almost finished they'll move on. This means the cattle don't ruin the pasture by eating every scrap of grass, and the grass will grow back again when the next rains come.

The Masai manage the land very carefully, because the lives of their cattle depend on it. Pastures – where good grass grows – are set aside for different cattle at different times of the year and plans can be changed according to the amount of rain and the quality of the grass. In this way, the Masai don't spoil the land by overusing it. Today, people are buying up land and as less and less is free for pasture, overgrazing has started to become a problem.

Cattle help the Masai to stay together

Traditionally the Masai didn't live in one fixed place. Instead they travelled through some of the wildest country in Africa in family groups, seeking pasture for their animals. As they travelled, their traditions and customs were very important in keeping alive their sense of what it meant to be a Masai.

Cattle play a big part in Masai customs. Men give cattle as presents; the number of cattle a man owns shows how rich he is and he pays for his wedding with cattle. Cattle are also a kind of social security. If a family loans cattle when they are rich, if they become poor for any reason they can ask for their cattle back, knowing that their earlier **generosity** will be remembered.

Cattle play an important part in Masai ceremonies.

Masai kill cattle at important ceremonies, and if a Masai has done something wrong, he or his clan will hand over cattle as a way of saying sorry.

The Masai use cattle hides for mattresses, floor mats, rope, sandals and pouches for knives. They drink cows' milk or make it into yoghurt and even use cattle urine as a simple **disinfectant**.

Junior elders prepare for a feast.

13

Childhood

Small boys and girls live in their mother's house and play outside in the common space belonging to the enkang, or **homestead**. When they are six or seven, they are usually sent out during the day to herd the sheep or goats.

The Masai do things in "age groups". For men in particular, the other men of their age are like their family and the friendships they make in the group last a lifetime.

A boy will pass through each of the important stages in his life with the other boys in his group, although these days, the Masai are keen for their children to get a good education and boys spend less time as warriors than in the past.

Young warrior

The first big life stage comes when a boy is about thirteen or fourteen, and he becomes a moran or junior warrior. Once a boy has become a moran, he no longer lives at home. He goes with the other boys of his age to a group homestead, which the boys usually build themselves, called a manyatta. This is good training for survival as the boys learn to look after themselves and to work together. The morani must serve the clan and in the past would provide the fighting force if there was a war.

At this point, a young Masai's life must seem very good as he has as much freedom as he wants. He grows his hair and will probably spend a lot of time plaiting it into different styles. He can dance, make friends and travel wherever he likes and other Masai will give him food and shelter – because their own sons will also be in the same situation. In return, he must take most of the cattle to the grazing grounds, which may be far from his homestead, and defend the clan at all times.

Masai warriors are famous for their strength and agility, and a favourite competition is the jumping dance called aduni. The young men jump on the spot to see who can leap the highest. As one young man put it, "The higher I jump, the taller I will stand with my tribe."

warriors dancing the aduni

Settling down: the eunoto ceremony

When a group of morani are in their early twenties, they go through the ceremony of eunoto which is one of the most important moments in a man's life. This is when the senior elders decide that it's time for the young warriors to become junior elders. In the past, young men had to kill a lion before they could become junior elders. Today this is forbidden, unless they or their cattle are in danger. However, there's still great competition for the honour of wearing a lion's mane and a Masai who has killed a lion is regarded with great respect.

During the ceremony, the warriors decorate themselves with chalk. This **symbolises** the milk which they get from the cattle. Milk is usually a part of celebration and ceremony. They also paint themselves with red **ochre**.

The ceremony will last for several days with a great deal of singing and dancing, and the Masai will kill a cow or a goat for the feast.

young warriors at the eunoto ceremony

At the end of the ceremony, a moran's mother shaves off his long hair. This is a sad moment in a young man's life, because it marks the time when he gives up his carefree life as a moran for the responsibilities of a junior elder.

After the ceremony, the man is allowed to marry and he can own cattle.

Senior elder

One of the important things about Masai life is that each age group makes decisions amongst themselves and every junior elder will give his opinion. However, each group has a spokesperson, someone they all respect, who gives the decisions of the group to the Council of Elders.

After about ten years as a junior elder, together with the rest of his group a man will become a senior elder and may join the Council of Elders, called enkiguena. In the shade of an enormous African fig tree, the senior elders will often sit, discussing the affairs of the whole clan. According to one elder, "Our heritage, our customs and our way of life, this is the gift we give to our children. It is the knowledge of what it means to be Masai."

23

The laibon

Each clan usually has a laibon who chooses the best time for ceremonies. Everyone turns to him for advice. He is a priest and spiritual guide, handing down to his successor all the stored wisdom of the clan.

a laibon

The laibon is also a healer and the Masai are famous for their knowledge of **medicinal** herbs. Often a laibon will sell these herbs at the local market and give advice about sickness.

It is difficult for the Masai when the authority of the laibon is challenged. Today, when there are arguments over modern laws, the Masai often lose.

Masai women

Masai women own their houses and are responsible for the daily care of the sheep, goats and perhaps a couple of donkeys. They look after the children and fetch the water. Masai women may walk 16 kilometres each day to collect water from the nearest stream or spring. They also look after sick animals.

They prepare all the food and collect firewood because it is traditional for Masai women to keep a fire burning in their houses from the time they marry. The fire keeps everyone warm during the cooler seasons and the smoke also helps to keep flies and other insects away.

Today, international health organisations are encouraging Masai to cook vegetables, and to eat a wider variety of food. Unfortunately, this means more cooking on an open fire and Masai homes have become dangerously smoky because they aren't designed for this. Chest infections are common.

This woman is sterilizing a calabash bottle with a burning stick to make sure it's clean and ready to hold milk or water.

Although women can't own cattle, they milk the cows and look after the calves until they are strong enough to live outside the enkang.

The Masai home: the enkang

The enkang is a group of loaf-shaped houses inside a fence made from thorny acacia branches. The fence is set up to keep out wild animals and bandits and the Masai bring their cows, sheep and goats inside it in the evening. Baby animals are usually kept inside the houses.

Each enkang has several families in it and each wife has her own house, called an enkaji. One of a Masai woman's proudest moments is when she builds her first house. It's her responsibility to make sure that it's watertight and that she has plugged all the holes with mud and dung. A Masai home is not meant to be permanent and every few years or so the women will move the enkang to a new place. It's usually the women who decide this and it will probably not be far. The women explain with a laugh that they move when the dung heap from the animals inside the **enclosure** gets too high!

The new enkaji

A woman gathers her friends and relations together to help build a new enkaji and it usually turns into a celebration.

- First the women put thick branches into the ground in an oval shape.
- Then these are bent over and tied together with leather rope.
- More branches are used to mark out two or three rooms.
- Next the women weave smaller twigs and branches in between the thicker poles.
- Finally, they cover everything with mud, ash and cow dung, and this bakes almost as hard as cement in the hot sun.

An enkaji is usually only about three metres wide, five metres long and one and a half metres tall, so adults cannot stand upright inside. It has a small doorway that is protected on the inside with a wall, so that the dusty winds don't blow in. The bed is a wooden frame about 20 centimetres high, covered with several cow hides. A small hole in the roof lets out smoke from the fire. The second room is often used as a pen for young animals.

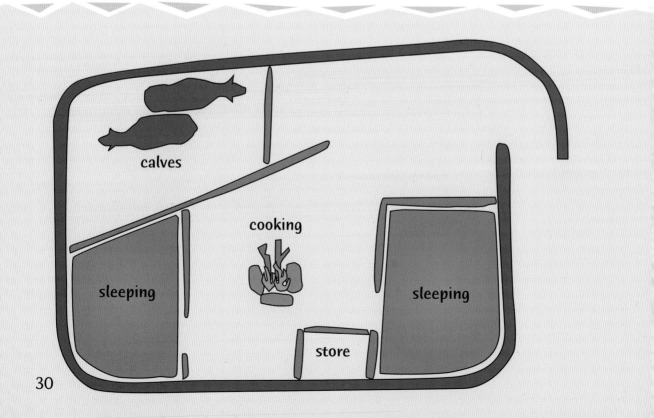

Daily life inside a Masai enkang

Dawn

At first light, the family sit huddled together on their three-legged wooden stools, sipping sweet tea and chatting. It's dark and smoky inside the house and the snuffles of the young calves next door can be heard as they wake too. A thin curl of smoke rises up to the low roof and slips out through a small hole. Outside in the early morning mist, a group of women are already milking. They talk quietly to each cow as the milk splashes into a calabash bowl.

Fact

A calabash is a kind of fruit which has a very hard skin when it dries out. The Masai use it as a bottle or cut it into bowls.

This woman is cooking indoors on an open fire.

Looking after the animals

A couple of flies buzz lazily. They will be joined by many thousands more as the sun gets higher and the heat rises. Some children have come outside and are sweeping the earth in front of the house with bunches of twigs. An older girl and her mother have already left the enkang to fetch water, carrying big plastic cans.

These women are setting out on the long walk to fetch water.

Now the milking is finished and two boys are taking the cows out of the enkang to find grass. Most of the cattle are with the young warriors in the distant pastures, but some are needed at the enkang. Soon, more children will take the sheep and the goats out of their pens and follow the cows. The Masai don't take the smaller animals to the pastures until the dew has dried on the grass because they believe it will make them sick.

A woman comes out of her house with the heavy hide of a newly killed **steer**, and begins to scrape away the bits of skin and flesh that are still sticking to it.

Her husband sets out for the market. He's going to meet a friend from another clan and arrange the sale of some cattle. It's very important for the Masai to keep up links with other groups and friendships are cemented by a system of exchanging and selling cattle.

These Masai women are rolling out a cow hide.

Trading

Later in the day, the women settle down in the shade of a thorn tree with some beadwork. They are making a gorgeous necklace for one of the girls who will be married shortly. Beads are a sign of wealth and they are keen that their family will look as good as possible.

Little girls love to wear beads.

They are also making necklaces and belts which they hope to sell to traders and tourists who will give them money in exchange for goods. With the money, the women will buy tea, sugar, salt and perhaps maize flour at the stores which are several hours walk away. Today, some of the wealthier Masai have cars, but many still walk everywhere or ride a bicycle.

Evening

In the evening, the cows return. Some of the men look over the animals to check that they have all returned safely and that none is sick or injured.

One man chooses a cow and ties a leather strap round its neck. He tightens it. The cow looks at him and gives a low mooing sound as the big vein in its neck swells slightly. Then the man takes out a small bow and an arrow with a sharp metal tip and fires the arrow at the cow's vein. Quickly, he catches the cow's blood in a calabash and when the calabash is half full, he lets go of the leather strap. The blood stops flowing immediately, and the cow walks away as if nothing has happened. Then the man takes a stick and stirs the blood, so that some of it clots on the stick. He takes that away to roast on the fire. The thinner blood will be drunk mixed with milk.

The children run to their mothers' huts for a meal of milk, yoghurt and maize. If it's a special day, or if there are visitors, someone will kill a goat, cut it into four or five large chunks and roast it over an open fire. The men will get the best parts of the meat, the liver and the rump and the fat, but everyone will eat the rest of the goat, even the intestines.

In the evening the animals are driven back from the pastures to the enkang. Inside the thorn fence they are safe from rustlers and wild animals.

The future

The Masai are proud of their traditions, but their traditional way of life is becoming more difficult. Their land is valuable for tourism, agriculture and for building plots, and little by little, the Masai are being persuaded to sell. Unfortunately, once they've sold land, they can no longer travel over it in the way they've always done, following the rains and the good grass for their cattle. But the land is too dry for large numbers of cattle to live in one spot all year. Cattle get sick and die, and as cattle represent wealth for the Masai, losing cattle is the same as losing their money.

These young Masai warriors are about to become junior elders. Traditions like this are under threat as the young Masai drift to the towns in search of work and education.

Gradually the Masai are settling in villages and growing crops. Some are glad of the chance to put down roots and get a good education. But others are worried. In the past, the elders had all the knowledge their people needed, but the younger men are no longer under their control. Some find work as rangers in the game parks or work in the tourist camps and lodges, but others drift into the towns where it can be hard to find jobs and where they don't have their families to support them.

The rich wildlife of East Africa brings many visitors from across the world and game parks have been created to protect this wildlife. Here, the Masai can't graze their cattle freely in the way they used to, but they can earn a living in the tourist industry. Tourists are interested in the Masai way of life, and will pay to see them perform traditional songs and dances.

Today the Masai are looking out beyond the game parks and want to educate their children to play a part in their changing world. As they come to rely less and less on their cattle for their livelihood, it's hard for them to keep up old traditions in the same way.

Education is very important to the Masai and these days everyone wants their children to go to primary school.

An old Masai saying is: "It takes one day to pull down a house, but to make a new one takes many months. If we leave our way of life to start a new one, it will take a thousand years to rebuild."

The challenge for the Masai is to find a way to belong to the modern world without losing their traditions and their pride in being Masai.

Glossary

authorities   government bodies that have the power to say what people can and can't do

ceremonies   special events that often mark particular stages in life and involve many members of a family or community

clan   a group of people who are all related to each other or live together in the same area

disinfectant   a liquid that kills germs and prevents the spread of illness

eland   the largest type of African antelope

enclosure   a piece of land with a fence round it

generosity   willingness to share or give away your possessions

homestead   a group of buildings, including a house, and the land that surrounds it

medicinal   to do with medicine and healing

ochre   a natural earth with a red or orange colour, often used in dye and paint

reputation   an opinion or belief held by a lot of people about someone; it isn't necessarily true or accurate

steer   a bullock

symbolises   represents; stands for

Index

A day in the life of a Masai child

Early morning

"We wake up at dawn. Mum rekindles the fire and makes sweet tea for us to drink. In the next room, the calves are waking up."

Morning

"I help Mum fetch water, while my sister sweeps the earth in front of the house with a bunch of twigs. As soon as the dew has dried, my oldest brother takes the cows out to find pasture. I follow with the sheep and goats. One of my sisters stays behind to help with the baby. My little brother helps to look after the new calf."

Afternoon

"We watch over the cows, goats and sheep in the pastures."

"We make sure the animals are back at the enkang before sunset."

Evening

"We play together until it's time to eat our evening meal. Usually we have milk, yoghurt and maize, but if it's a special occasion we'll have roast goat."

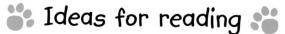 Ideas for reading

Written by Linda Pagett B.Ed (hons), M.Ed
Lecturer and Educational Consultant

Learning objectives: identify different types of text; identify features of non fiction texts; understand and use the terms fact and opinion; use and reflect on some ground rules for dialogue

Curriculum links: Geography: Knowledge and understanding of places; Citizenship: developing good relationships and respecting the differences between people

Interest words: authorities, ceremonies, clan, eland, enclosure, homestead, ochre, steer, laibon

Resources: whiteboard

Getting started

This book can be read over two or more guided reading sessions..

- Ask the children some of the features of non-fiction texts (*contents page, glossary, photographs*) and list these on whiteboard. Check to see which features are in this book. Introduce the term report and revise features such as non-chronological writing.

- Discuss the title and purpose of this book and how features such as headings, glossary and illustrations help understanding and information retrieval.

- Read the glossary together and discuss unfamiliar words or concepts.

- Read the first chapter together and demonstrate to children the difference between fact and opinion (e.g. *Women wear necklaces – fact; necklaces are gorgeous – opinion.*)

Reading and responding

- Encourage the children to read a chapter silently to themselves and be aware of what's fact and what's opinion.

- Discuss in turn what facts and opinions the children have read.

- Ask if there is any information they have found in the pictures which is not in the text.